Looking at Senses

David Suzuki

with BARBARA HEHNER

John Wiley & Sons, Inc.
New York • Chichester • Brisbane • Toronto • Singapore

In recognition of the importance of preserving what has been written, it is a policy of John Wiley & Sons, Inc., to have books of enduring value published in the United States printed on acid-free paper, and we exert our best efforts to that end.

*Published in Canada by Stoddart Publishing Co., Limited
First U.S. edition published by John Wiley & Sons, Inc., in 1991
Illustrations © 1986, 1991 by Peter Grau*

This publication is designed to provide accurate and authoritative information in regard to the subject matter covered. It is sold with the understanding that the publisher is not engaged in rendering legal, accounting, or other professional service. If legal advice or other expert assistance is required, the services of a competent professional person should be sought.
From a Declaration of Principles jointly adopted by a Committee of the American Bar Association and a Committee of Publishers.

Library of Congress Cataloging-in-Publication Data

Suzuki, David T., 1936–
    Looking at senses / David Suzuki with Barbara Hehner.
        p.   cm. — (David Suzuki's Looking at Series)
    Includes index.
    Summary: Tells about the common human senses such as sight, hearing, taste, and touch, and also about the more uncommon ones, such as ESP.
    ISBN 0-471-54751-4 (lib. ed.)
    ISBN 0-471-54048-X (paper)
    1. Senses and sensation—Juvenile literature.   [1. Senses and sensation.]   I. Hehner, Barbara.   II. Title.
QP434.S89   1991
612.8—dc20   90-10772
                                                  AC

Printed in the United States of America

10 9 8 7 6 5 4 3 2 1

Table of Contents

Introduction 5

CHAPTERS

Senses in Your Skin 7
How Do You Smell Things? 17
How Do You Taste Things? 28
How Do You See? 36
More about Colors and Light 48
How Do You Hear? 59
More about Sounds 68
Some Other Senses—and ESP 79
Inventions to Stretch Our Senses 87

Index 96

To Tara and Rick, with love

AN IMPORTANT NOTE FOR KIDS AND GROWNUPS
You will see this ✋ warning sign on some of the **Things to Do** in this book. It means that an adult should help out. The project may use some boiling water or something might need to be cut with a knife. Everyone needs to be extra careful. Most grownups will want to get involved in these projects anyway—why should kids have all the fun?

Introduction

Have you ever tried to catch a dragonfly with your hands? I always missed, and I used to think the dragonfly was laughing at me as it darted quickly away. Dragonflies have special eyes that are very sensitive to movement, which makes them difficult to catch. Have you ever snuck up beside a cat when it was snoozing in the sun, and snapped your fingers to see what would happen? Its ears suddenly twitched, didn't they? This is because a cat has a very keen sense of hearing. And what happens when a dog smells the scent of another animal such as a dog, cat or rabbit? It gets excited, and runs around sniffing the scent trail the other animal has left behind. The dog, the cat and the dragonfly, like all animals and insects, use their *senses* to find out about the world around them.

You depend on *your* senses, too, to tell you what is going on all around you. Your nose tells you when Mom is baking a turkey or an apple pie. Your eyes let you check for cars before you cross a street. Your fingertips let you know whether the bath water is too hot or too cold. You know — without looking — which way is up, because you have balance organs built into your ears. You prefer certain things to eat because you have taste buds in your mouth. Like all other living creatures, you have special organs to sample the world around you.

Our sense organs are marvelous structures. People often refer to parts of our bodies as if they are machines. I think that's wrong, though.

No machine can come close to doing what our organs do. For one thing, if they are damaged, they can often repair themselves. Do you know of any machine that can do that?

We often take our senses for granted because we don't have to think about using them. And sometimes we subject them to pretty tough wear and tear. Children and teenagers sometimes like to listen to music at "full blast." Ears are sensitive, though, and can be permanently damaged by loud noises. Bright lights can damage the eyes; too much sunlight harms the skin; and many chemicals can hurt the nose and tongue. Your senses are a wonderful gift, so take good care of them.

DAVID SUZUKI

Senses in Your Skin

Oh, ya gotta have skin
It's what keeps your insides in . . .

These are the first two lines of a silly song I learned as a kid. It shows the way we usually think of our skin—as a big bag that holds us together. But skin does a lot more than that. Skin protects our bodies from bacteria and other invisible enemies. It's waterproof and it blocks the burning rays of the sun. It sweats to cool us down when we're getting too hot. It is also our biggest sense organ.

People often say that they have five senses. The first four are sight, hearing, smell and taste. "Sense of touch" is usually counted as the fifth sense. As you'll see, though, there are many senses in your skin.

The top layer of your skin is called the *epidermis*. This is the layer that protects your body. In some places, like the soles of your feet, it is thick and tough. In other places, like the skin around your eyes, it is very thin. Just under the the epidermis is a thicker layer of skin called the *dermis*. The dermis contains blood vessels, hair roots and sweat glands. It also contains a network of nerves.

Did you know that all your senses need nerves to work properly? Your ears, for example, are special sense organs that can pick up sounds. But nerves—like telephone wires—carry the message back to your brain. Until the message reaches your brain, you don't "hear" anything. Your eyes, your nose, and your tongue, too, are joined by nerves to your brain. Your brain sorts out all the sense messages and decides what they mean.

The nerves in your skin have different special endings, depending on what kind of message they are going to carry. These nerve endings are called *sense receptors*. Your skin has many different kinds of sense receptors.

Each hair on your skin has a *touch receptor* wrapped around its root. If an ant starts to crawl up your arm, it brushes against the tiny hairs on your skin. Even without looking, you can feel where it is and flick it away. Other touch receptors in your skin can feel pressure (pushing).

You also have *temperature receptors*. There are separate ones for hot and for cold. These receptors keep you from drinking cocoa that's too hot and from swimming in a lake that's too cold. Your hot and cold receptors can't tell you the temperature the way a thermometer can, though. They just tell you if a thing is hotter or colder against your skin than what was there before. Suppose you've been in an overheated store. You might step out onto a sunny street and find it cool. But if you're coming out of an air-conditioned restaurant, you might find the same street very hot.

When you first get into a swimming pool, your receptors might report that it's *coooold!* After a few minutes, though, you feel as if the water has "warmed up." The water temperature hasn't changed; instead, your receptors got used to the temperature. After a while, they stopped sending messages about it.

Pain receptors are different. They won't stop sending messages as long as something is hurting your body. If you have a pulled muscle, the pain makes you rest. If you have a cut on the sole of your foot, the pain warns you so that you can put a bandage on it.

People who study pain used to think that it was felt by the touch and temperature receptors. For instance, a bruise was "too much pressure." A burn was "too much heat." However, they discovered that pain has its own receptors. If fact, there are even different receptors for different *kinds* of pain. For instance, burns are felt by one kind of pain receptor, and cuts are felt by another kind.

As you can see, your skin puts you in touch with the world around you in many different ways!

Get the Point?

Find some of the sense receptors in your skin.

What You Need:
a fine-tip pen
a sheet of paper
pens or pencils in four
    different colors
a short piece of thread
a pushpin or straight pin
a metal fork
an ice cube
a cup of hot water

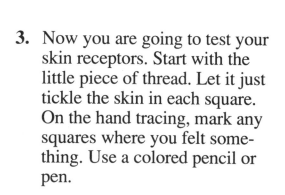

What to Do:

1. Use a fine-tip pen to draw a square on the palm of your hand. It should be about 2 inches (5 cm) square. Now draw lines across the square to divide it into many tiny squares.

2. On a piece of paper, trace the outline of your hand. Now draw a square on the hand tracing, the same size as the one on your hand. Divide it into the same number of small squares.

3. Now you are going to test your skin receptors. Start with the little piece of thread. Let it just tickle the skin in each square. On the hand tracing, mark any squares where you felt something. Use a colored pencil or pen.

4. Touch the tip of the pin to each square. (*Don't* break the skin. This is a test, not a torture!) Mark your tracing, using a different color.

5. Hold the prong of a fork against the ice cube until it is very cold. Touch it to your skin. After every three or four squares, chill the fork again. Mark your tracing in another color.

6. Now put the fork in the hot water until it is hot. (*Don't* use boiling water.) Touch a prong to your skin. Reheat the fork when it cools off. Mark your tracing in another color.

7. On the paper you can see where some of your touch, pain, cold and hot receptors are. Does your palm have more of one kind than it has of another?

8. Try this again on the back of your hand. (When I took the test, I couldn't feel the thread *anywhere* on the palm of my hand. But I could certainly feel it tickle the back of my hand.)

AMAZING FACT

The Back of Your Hand—An Unknown Land

Have you ever heard the expression, "I know this place like the back of my hand"? Perhaps you've used it yourself. But just how well *do* you know the back of your hand? Take a look. Just some skin, a few hairs, and a couple of veins, you say? The wonders of the back of your hand are too small for your eyes to see. A piece of skin on the back of your hand just ½ inch (1 cm) square can contain about: 15 hairs, 150 sweat glands, 2 oil glands, over 1½ yards (1 m) of blood vessels, 6½ yards (6 m) of nerves, 4500 nerve endings, 300 pain sensors, 3 cold sensors, 18 heat sensors, and 38 pressure sensors.

How Much Touch?

On some parts of your body, touch receptors can be as much as 2 inches (5 cm) apart. Other places on your skin are much more sensitive. Find out how touchy you are!

What You Need:

a piece of stiff cardboard, about 4 inches x 1½ inches
  (10 cm x 4 cm)
a pen or pencil
2 straight pins
a blindfold
a partner

What to Do:

1. Mark the piece of cardboard as shown. Leave space at each end so you can hold the cardboard.

2. Stick two pins through the cardboard, 2 inches (5 cm) apart.

3. Blindfold a friend. Press the pins *gently* against a friend's skin at the following places: palm of hand, calf of leg, inside of forearm and (if your friend is wearing thin clothing) middle of back.

4. Can your friend feel one pin or two? If your friend can feel only one pin, it means that his or her touch receptors are farther apart than the pins are. Keep a record of what your friend says.

5. Now try again with the pins 1½ inches (4 cm) apart. Any change in the results? Keep trying the pins closer and closer together. Where is your friend's skin most sensitive?

6. Trade places with your friend, and find out how sensitive your own skin is.

Temperature Trick

You dip a toe into the pool and say it's too cold. Your friend, who's been swimming for a while, says it's warm. Who's right?

What You Need:
three bowls
water

What to Do:

1. Fill one bowl with icewater. Fill the second bowl with hot tap water, but not so hot that it hurts to put your hand in it.

2. Fill the third bowl with *tepid* tap water— that means water that feels neither hot nor cold to your hand.

3. Line up the three bowls with the tepid water in the middle. Put your right index finger (the one next to your thumb) in the icewater. Put your left index finger in the hot water. After a minute or so, one finger will feel quite cold and the other finger will feel quite hot. Now put both fingers in the middle bowl.

4. How does the water feel to the two fingers? What does this tell you about how temperature receptors can be fooled?

5. Take the two fingers out of the water. After a few minutes, put them back in the tepid water. Does this tell you why the pool water feels warmer after a while?

6. You can try the activity again with two different fingers of *one hand*. What happens?

Weird Wetness

Your hands won't touch the water—but they'll feel "wet" anyway.

What You Need:
rubber gloves
a large mixing bowl or
    bucket containing ice water
a large mixing bowl or
    bucket containing warm water

What to Do:

1. Put on the rubber gloves.

2. Put your hands in the cold water. The rubber gloves keep your hands dry, but do they *feel* dry?

3. Now try putting your hands in the warm water. Is the feeling as strange as it was in the cold water?

How does "wetness" feel to skin? It feels cold and it feels like pressure all over the skin. If your sense receptors feel both of these things, they will send a "wet" message back to your brain.

Fingertip Reading

You have about 100 "touch receptors" on the tip of each finger. Many blind people use their sensitive fingertips to read. Their books are printed in a special code called *braille*. In braille, patterns of raised dots stand for the different letters of the alphabet. (There are braille dots for numbers and punctuation, too.) Braille was invented over 150 years ago by Louis Braille, a blind teacher in France. Today, blind people can read braille books, use braille watches and thermometers—and even play a game of braille Scrabble!

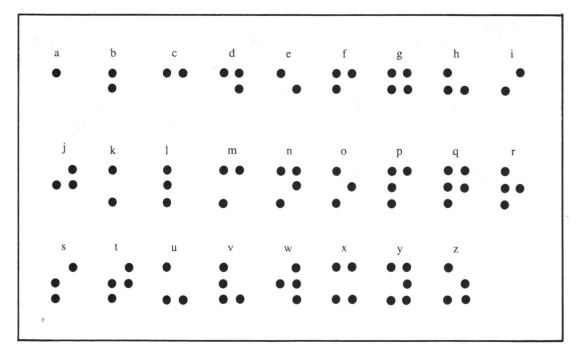

If this were a real braille book, the dots would be raised so that your fingertips could feel them.

How Do You Smell Things?

*A*n ant is crawling along a path. Suddenly it meets a large enemy ant. The first ant hurries back to its nest. The ants guarding the nest know that it's safe to let this ant in. Inside, the ant spreads the news that the nest is going to be attacked. All the ants scurry around, getting ready to defend themselves.

Ants don't have voices. They can't see very well. Instead, they tell each other things with smells. All ants from the same nest have the same smell. An enemy ant smells different. When an ant is frightened, it gives off an "alarm" smell. This tells the other ants that there is danger. In fact, ants have a whole "language" of smells. It's their most important sense.

Being able to smell is important to us, too. Every so often, people's lives are saved by their sense of smell. They throw away rotten-smelling food that could poison them. Or they smell smoke and escape from a fire. Maybe you can think of a time when an odor gave you a warning. Most of the time, though, you probably don't think about your sense of smell. You learn much more about the world from your eyes and ears.

The part of your nose that smells things is very small. It's a little patch about the size of a postage stamp, high up in your nose. It's covered with a liquid called *mucus*. This little wet patch contains millions of very tiny nerve cells, with even tinier hairs waving from them.

Everything in the world is made of extremely small particles called *molecules*. They can only be seen by the most powerful electron microscopes. Some of the molecules that make up a thing may break loose

from it. Suppose you're holding an orange in your hand. Molecules from the orange are always breaking off and sailing into the air. When you breathe in, the air carries some of the odor molecules up into your nose. They're caught by the tiny hairs of the nerve cells and dissolve (break down) in the liquid. Special nerves then carry an orange "smellagram" to your brain. You find yourself thinking what a delicious snack that orange is going to make.

You may also find yourself remembering your very first day of school, and how excited you were. You opened your brand new lunchbox— and found an orange. This is an interesting thing about your sense of smell. Smells can be linked with very powerful feelings and memories. Nerve messages about smell go to a deep and mysterious part of the brain. It's far away from the part of the brain that controls thinking and talking. But it's close to the parts that affect our feelings.

Have you ever arrived home when cake or bread was just out of the oven? You tip back your head and sniff deeply. What a great smell! By the time you've taken off your boots and hung up your coat, though, the aroma seems much weaker. After a little while, you can't smell it at all. If your nerve cells receive too many of the cake molecules, they get *fatigued* (tired out). They'll be able to smell other things, but they won't be able to smell the cake till they've had a rest from it.

You can never hang onto smells. You can never quite remember them when they've gone. You can never quite describe them to someone else. Yet you wouldn't want to be without them.

Roses for Noses

You can make sweet-scented rosewater as a present for someone — or to sprinkle on yourself!

What You Need:

rose petals
small, clean bottles with screw-on tops
a heatproof bowl
a saucepan with a tight-fitting lid (big enough to hold the heatproof bowl)
a bowl or jug with a spout
a strainer
a funnel

What to Do:

1. Pick roses on a sunny morning, as soon as the dew has dried off them. (Ask permission *before* you pick!)

2. Strip the petals from the roses. (Watch out for thorns.) Throw away any spotted or torn petals. Put the best petals in the heatproof bowl.

3. Hold the bowl under the tap. Pour on cold water until the petals are just covered.

4. Fill the saucepan about one-quarter full of water. Put the heatproof bowl in the saucepan, and put the lid on the saucepan.

5. Put the saucepan on a stove burner. Heat the saucepan until the water in the petal bowl is *almost* boiling. (The water should be starting to move, but not bubbling hard.)

6. Turn off the stove burner. Move the saucepan to a cold

burner, still with its lid on. Let the water cool for about half an hour.

7. Remove the bowl from the saucepan. Hold the sieve over the bowl with the spout. Pour the water and petals into the sieve.

8. Keep the rosewater that drains into the bowl and throw out the petals.

9. Pour the rosewater into small bottles and screw their caps on tightly. Use the rosewater within a day or two—its sweet smell turns into a very bad smell if it is kept too long!

An Orange-Clove Pomander Ball

These oranges are for sniffing, not eating.
They make drawers and closets smell spicy-fresh.

What You Need:
1 cup (250 mL) whole cloves
    (sold in a grocery store)
an orange
ground cinnamon
a small paper bag
2 pieces of ribbon, 1½ inches (4 cm)
    wide, long enough to tie
    around the orange
1 piece of ribbon, ¼ inch (6 mm)
    wide and 6 inches (15 cm) long

What to Do:

1. Push the pointed ends of the cloves into the orange skin. (If the skin is too thick, use a small skewer or nail to make the holes first.) Cover the orange with cloves.

2. Put 1 tablespoon (15 mL) of cinnamon in the bag. Hold the top of the bag shut. Give the bag a couple of shakes.

3. Take the orange out of the bag. Hold it over the sink and blow off any loose cinnamon.

4. Tie the two wide ribbons around the orange as shown in the drawing.

5. Slip the narrow ribbon under the knot made by the other ribbons. Tie it in a loop. Now the pomander ball can be hung in a clothes closet.

After a while, the orange will get smaller and harder—but it will still smell great!

Gee Whiz—It's Fizz!

The next time you take a bath, feel a fizz against your skin—and breathe in a sweet scent, too.

What You Need:

¾ cup (175 mL) baking soda
½ cup (125 mL) cream of tartar   } you can buy these
2 tablespoons (30 mL) cornstarch   } at a grocery store
a measuring cup
measuring spoons
a few drops of perfume or cologne (ask permission before using)
    or a few drops of peppermint extract or almond extract
a glass jar with a tight-fitting lid

What to Do:

1. Measure the baking soda and put it in the jar. Do the same with the cream of tarter.

2. Spoon the cornstarch into the jar. Stir the mixture with a spoon to get out any lumps.

3. Add a few drops of perfume or extract. Stir the mixture again.

4. Close the jar tightly.

5. The next time you have a bath, add a couple of spoonfuls of bath fizz . The mixture will make hundreds of tiny tingly bubbles.

SOMETHING TO DO

Soup's On!

Aah!—home-made minestrone, a hearty soup. While it's simmering, it fills the house with a mouth-watering aroma. And then you get to eat it!

What You Need:
measuring cups
measuring spoons
a big stirring spoon
paring knife
cutting board
vegetable peeler
a big soup pot with a lid

Ingredients for Soup:
1 pound (500 g) of stewing beef, cut into
    small pieces (The butcher at the supermarket
    can cut it for you.)
1 large celery stalk, with leaves
1 large onion
1 clove of garlic (if you like garlic; otherwise leave it out)
19 ounce (540 mL) can of tomatoes
2 to 3 cups (500 to 750 mL) of frozen vegetables—anything you have at
    your house, such as peas and carrots, string beans, and corn
1 cup (250 mL) uncooked elbow macaroni (you can also use spaghetti
    broken into short pieces)
½ teaspoon (2 mL) salt
¼ teaspoon (1 mL) pepper

What to Do:

1. Ask for help to chop up the celery, onion and garlic. Don't use the paring knife without permission. First wash the celery and chop it into small pieces.

2. Then peel the skin off the onion and chop it into small pieces. (Did the onion make you cry? The sharp odor given off by onion makes tears roll down some people's faces!) Chop the clove of garlic into little pieces.

3. Put the big soup pot on the stove. Put the beef pieces and the pieces of onion, celery and garlic into the pot. Pour 8 cups (2 L) of water over them.

4. Turn the burner to high until the water begins to boil (roll and bubble). Then turn the heat down to low. Let the soup simmer for 2 hours with the pot lid on. (The soup is simmering when it is steaming and moving a little, but not bubbling hard as it does when it boils.)

5. Check the soup every 20 minutes or so. If some scum is collecting on the surface, skim it off with your stirring spoon.

6. Add the frozen vegetables and canned tomatoes. If the soup seems too thick, add another 1 cup (250 mL) water. Cover the soup again and let it simmer for about 15 minutes.

7. Add the macaroni, salt and pepper. Cover the soup again and simmer for 15 minutes. Now take the lid off and breathe the rich aroma of your soup. It tastes just as good as it smells, so serve it up!

World's Champion Sniffer

The world's best sense of smell belongs to an insect. The male Indian moon moth can smell a female moth who is almost 7 miles (up to 11 km) away from him! The female moth (like many other insects) gives off special chemicals call *pheromones*. Other creatures can't smell these chemicals. This way, she can send out a long-distance message without telling her enemies—who might make a snack of her — where she is.

P.S. The moth doesn't actually "sniff" at all. He doesn't have a nose! Instead, he uses his antennae to pick up smells.

Truffle Snufflers

Some of the most valuable noses in the world belong to—pigs! Delicious fungi called truffles grow in some parts of Europe. But they grow on tree roots below the ground, where people can't find them. So, people have trained pigs to sniff out these fancy fungi. Why go to all this trouble? Truffles are considered such a special treat that they can be sold for over $600 a pound ($1300 a kg)!

An Amazingly Talented Nose

It's hard to imagine a more amazing nose than the one an elephant has. An elephant's nose—which we usually call a trunk—can be about 8 feet (over 2 m) long. The elephant can suck up about 5 quarts (almost 5 L) of water in its trunk. It then sprays the water into its mouth for a drink, or over its back for a shower. The elephant's trunk can pick up something as tiny as a pencil, or a huge, heavy log. The elephant can also use its trunk to scratch an itchy ear or stroke its baby. Its trunk is used just like an ordinary animal nose too—for breathing and smelling!

How Do You Taste Things?

Aa-choo! You've got a *baad* cold. Your throat is sore, your eyes are watering, and your nose is all plugged up. Nothing seems like fun. Even your favorite snack — a big, juicy apple — doesn't taste the way it should. Do you know why?

Your blocked nose is the problem. It's hard to believe, but most of the "taste" of a food really comes from its smell. You can smell the food even after it's inside your mouth, because your nose and mouth are joined together where your throat begins. Your tongue can tell that you are licking an ice cream cone. But it's your nose that figures out you're having strawberry ice cream and not cherry. Your tongue can only detect *four* different tastes: sweet, sour, salty and bitter.

Stand in front of the mirror and stick out your tongue. Can you see a lot of little red bumps all over it? Inside these bumps are many tiny *taste buds*. You have about 3,000 of them. Taste buds are joined to nerves that carry taste messages to your brain.

Something else to notice about your tongue is that it's all wet. A dry tongue can't taste anything. You can prove this for yourself. Dry off the end of your tongue with a paper towel or handkerchief. Sprinkle a few grains of sugar on it. The sugar won't taste sweet until your *saliva* makes your tongue — and the sugar — wet. (Saliva is the special liquid in your mouth that helps you digest your food.)

Here's an amazing fact about your tongue that you can't see in the mirror. (You're probably tired of looking at your tongue sticking out, anyway!) Some taste buds are best at tasting sweet things. Some are best at tasting sour things. There are also special taste buds for salty and for bitter. They're grouped in different places on your tongue. Although you can't see where they are, you can find them. Can you think how? (See page 32 for a way to do it.)

Have you ever wondered why food seems to taste different to different people? Your best friend may love dill pickles. You think, how could anybody *like* that taste? Often, we like to eat what our families eat. If we have lots of roast beef, or vegetable curry, or raw fish when we're young, then these things probably taste good to us when we're grown up. It's just a matter of what we're used to.

Still, there are real differences in what people can taste. There's a chemical called PTC that tastes bitter to most people. But some people can't taste it at all.

The way people taste things also changes as they grow older. Babies and children seem to like much sweeter things than adults do. Here's something else. Your parents have fewer taste buds than you do. (And when you were a baby, you had more than you have now.) So, many foods have a stronger taste to you than they do to grownups. If you don't like broccoli now, take heart. You may love it when you are your parents' age!

There are still lots of mysteries about taste. Why is it that when we're hungry, food tastes better to us? Why does the way food looks change the way we think it tastes? In one test, people thought blue fried eggs tasted terrible — but the taste hadn't been changed, only the color. Even people who spend all their time studying taste aren't sure of the answers to these questions. Maybe you'll be the one to find out!

Take a Taste Test

Without your sense of smell, it's hard to tell foods apart.

What You Need:
a vegetable peeler
a paring knife
a potato
an apple
a pear
an onion
4 plates
a nose clip (the kind used for
    swimming)
a glass of water
a blindfold

What to Do:
1. Peel the apple, the potato and the pear. Cut them up into pieces of about the same size and shape. Cut a slice off the onion. Put the food on plates. (Put the onion in another room where your friend won't smell it.)

2. Blindfold a friend. Put a noseclip on your friend's nose. Put a piece of apple in your friend's mouth. Can your friend tell what it is?

3. Have your friend rinse out his or her mouth with water. Try again with pieces of potato and pear. Can your friend tell the difference between the two?

4. Remove the noseclip. With a sense of smell to help, your friend should have no trouble telling the three foods apart.

5. Now try this. Get the piece of onion. Hold it under your friend's nose while putting a little piece of apple in his or her mouth. What does your friend taste?

6. Trade places with your friend and try the taste test yourself.

Map Your Tongue

Can you taste sugar all over your tongue — or just on part of it? Find out for yourself how your tongue tastes sweet, salty, sour and bitter.

What You Need:
four small dishes
sugar, vinegar, salt
unsweetened grapefruit juice
cotton-tipped swab sticks
sheet of paper
four colored pencils

What to Do:
1. Put a little water into three of the dishes. Add 1 tablespoon (15 mL) of sugar (sweet) to the first dish. Add 1 teaspoon (5 mL) of salt to the second dish and 1 teaspoon (5 mL) of vinegar (sour) to the third. In the fourth dish, put a little unsweetened fresh grapefruit juice (bitter).

2. Draw a tongue diagram (like a big letter U) on a piece of paper.

3. Dip a swab stick in the vinegar water solution. Touch it to different parts of your tongue. Whenever you can taste sourness, mark the place on your tongue diagram with a colored pencil.

4. After testing the sour taste, rinse out your mouth very well with water. Then, using other swab sticks, try the same test for sweet, salty and bitter. Use different colored pencils to mark your tongue diagram.

5. When you're finished, you'll have a "map" of your tongue's taste buds.

   Most people taste sweetness more easily with the tips of their tongues. Did you? Where did you taste saltiness? Sourness? Bitterness?

Try this activity with a friend. Does your friend's tongue map look like yours?

Make It Sweeter—with Salt !

A tiny bit of salt makes sweet food taste sweeter—as you'll find out.

What You Need:
a small cantaloupe melon
a knife
2 plates
a salt shaker
pencil and paper
glasses of water
some friends or family
     to take the test

What to Do:

1. Slice the melon in halves. Cut up each half into bite-sized pieces. Put the pieces from each half on a plate.

2. *Lightly* sprinkle one plate of melon with salt. This is plate 1. Plate 2 stays unsalted. Eat a piece of melon from each plate, rinsing your mouth out in between. Which melon tastes sweeter to you?

3. Set out the plates of melon, along with a glass of water for each person you are going to test.

4. One at a time, bring your family or your friends over to the plates of melon . Give each person a piece from plate 1. Next, ask the person to rinse out his or her mouth with water. Then give the person a piece of melon from plate 2.

5. Ask which piece of melon tasted sweeter, the first or the second. Keep track of what people say on a sheet of paper. You can keep this up until you run out of melon pieces or people.

6. How many people thought the plate 1 melon pieces were sweeter? How many chose the pieces from plate 2? Did anybody say that a piece of melon tasted salty?

Sugar, Spice ... and Everything Nice

For thousands of years, people have been adding flavor to their food with spices. Many kids especially like nutmeg, so here is an easy recipe.

Nutmeg Eggnog

What You Need:
a mixing bowl
an egg beater
measuring spoons
measuring cup
two glasses
1 large egg
1 teaspoon (5 mL) sugar
½ teaspoon (2 mL) vanilla extract
1 cup (250 mL) cold milk
ground nutmeg

What to Do:
1. Break an egg into the bowl. Beat it with the egg beater until it is yellow and foamy.

2. Add the sugar and vanilla. Beat again.

3. Add the cupful of cold milk. Beat until the mixture is very foamy.

4. Pour the eggnog into two glasses. Sprinkle a little nutmeg (about ⅛ teaspoon or 0.5 mL) in each glass. Enjoy!

Toothpaste + Orange Juice = Yuk!

It's a school morning and you slept in. You gulp down your breakfast. Then you rush around, gathering up your books, pencil case, and lunch box. You remember to brush your teeth, and you're almost out the door when your dad says, "Wait—you forgot to drink your orange juice!" You fill your mouth with juice, and it tastes terrible! What happened? Toothpaste has some detergent in it, which keeps your taste buds from tasting sweetness for a while. So you can only taste the sour and bitter in your juice. The moral of this story is: remember to drink your juice *before* you brush your teeth.

Spaced Out Taste Buds

During the Gemini III space flight in 1965, astronaut John Young ate a corned beef sandwich. He had smuggled it aboard in his space suit. He just couldn't stand the official space meals: tubes of paste and little food cubes. Today, space food is much tastier. Astronauts dine on shrimp cocktail, beef and gravy, butterscotch pudding, and other treats. But they still complain — their food just doesn't taste the way it should.

NASA is trying to figure out what's wrong, since they want astronauts to be happy on long space flights. In October 1984, Canadian spaceman Marc Garneau did some sniff and taste tests on the *Challenger* space shuttle. (They were a lot like the ones in this book.) But the results were unclear. One theory is that zero gravity causes noses to get plugged up just like they do when you have a cold. (On page 28 , we explained why that spoils your sense of smell.) Or air currents in the spacecraft might not be spreading odors very well. Or weightlessness might mess up the way taste buds work. Although everyone agrees that flavors are different in space, no one really knows why.

How Do You See?

"Bye. See you tomorrow."
"Do you see what I mean?"
"We're going to see Grandma."
"See, I told you so."

*I*n everyday conversation, we use the word "see" all the time. Seeing is very important to us. Most human beings find out more about the world from their eyes than from any other sense organ.

Your eyes are two round balls, about 1 inch (24 mm) across. They are set in two holes in the front of your skull. The bone above the eyes juts out to protect them from being hit. Your eyebrows give a little padding to this bony ridge. (To help protect *it!*) They also keep sweat from dripping straight into your eyes.

Every couple of seconds, without needing to think about it, you blink. Your eyelids act like windshield wipers, cleaning the surface of your eyes. They also spread germ-killing tears across your eyes. Eyelashes on the edges of your lids flick away dirt. Your eyelids snap shut if something comes towards your face. When you sleep, your eyelids cover your eyes so that light and movement won't bother them and your eyes are kept moist.

There is a transparent ("see-through") bulge on the front of your eye called the *cornea*. The cornea lets light into your eye. The *iris* is behind the cornea. It is the colored part of your eye. In the center of the iris is the *pupil*. It looks like a black circle, but it's really an opening into your eye. It looks black because your eye is dark inside. The iris controls how much light gets into your eye. It has rings of muscle in it. When there's lots of light, the muscles squeeze in to make the pupil smaller. When it's dark, they let the pupil get bigger.

Stand in a dark room for a couple of minutes. Then turn on the light and quickly look in a mirror. You'll see your pupils getting smaller. Cats' eyes change more than yours do. Have you noticed that their pupils close down to slits in bright light?

Just inside the pupil is a clear *lens*. It is attached to muscles that pull it so that it changes shape. If you pay attention, you can feel these muscles at work. Hold a finger about 6 inches (15 cm) away from your face and look at it. Look at something far away. Look at your finger again. You can feel a little tug in your eyes as your lenses change shape.

The job of the lens is to bend the light coming into your eye. The lens makes the rays of light *focus* (form a clear image) on the inside back of your eye. Then nerves leading from your eye carry the image message to your brain. You'll learn more about what goes on inside your eye in the next chapter, *More about Colors and Light*.

Some people's lenses need help. They may bend the rays of light too much or too little. Then the images of things are fuzzy. Eyeglasses can change the way the light is bent, so that it focuses where it should: on the back of the eye.

Your eyes are about 2½ inches (6 cm) apart. This means that your two eyes see things from a slightly different angle. When you look at something, *two* images (a little bit different from each other) are sent to your brain. Then your brain puts them together into one picture. With two eyes, you can judge better how thick something is and how far away it is. Try playing catch with a friend with one eye closed. It's much harder to catch the ball!

Every year, many people lose their precious sight because of accidents. Take care to keep eye accidents from happening to you. Don't wave around a sharp, pointed stick or toy that could hurt your eyes. Never play with firecrackers or anything else that could explode and blind you. Wear safety goggles for woodworking and other hobbies where sharp bits can fly into your eyes. Take care — and enjoy the free show of shapes and colors the world gives you every day.

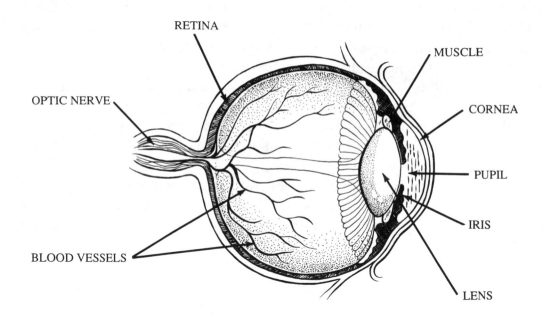

When One Eye Is Better than Two!

Some people find it tough to step on an escalator without tripping or falling. The lines on the moving steps confuse their eyes. Often one eye is focused on one line of the step, while the other eye is focused on another line. This throws off depth perception. (Sometimes a tiled floor can do the same thing to your eyes. All of a sudden, you feel like you are looking at *enormous* tiles, *far* below your feet. This happens when your two eyes are looking at different places in the design, but you think they're focusing on the same spot.) But what to do about the escalator problem? Simply close one eye when you get on.

What Makes Movies Move?

Do movies really move? Well, yes and no. The film certainly moves through the projector while you watch a movie. But if you hold up some film to the light, what do you see? Just a series of still pictures. The pictures are called frames. A special camera took the pictures, one after another very quickly, while the actors played their scenes.

It's really a trick of your eyes that makes movies seem to move. Your eyes hang onto the image of something for 1/16th of a second after you stop looking at it. This is called *persistence of vision*. Movies are usually projected at 24 frames per second. At that speed, your eyes hang onto one picture until the next picture is there. So you can't see the separate pictures of the actors. Instead, it looks like they are moving, just as they did when the movie was filmed.

Seeing Things (That Aren't There!)

You can trick your eyes into seeing impossible things.

I. A Hole in Your Hand

What You Need:
a piece of newspaper, about 9 inches (23 cm) square
scissors
tape

What to Do:

1. Roll the newspaper into a tube about 1 inch (3 cm) in diameter. Tape the loose edge of the newspaper in place.

2. Take the tube in your right hand. Hold it to your right eye so that you can see through it.

3. Hold your left hand in front of your left eye. Your palm should be facing you, about 4 inches (10 cm) away from your face.

4. Look straight ahead with both eyes. Can you believe your eyes? (Each eye is "telling the truth" about what it sees, but when your brain puts the two images together, it comes up with an illusion.)

II. A Finger Sausage

What to Do:
1. Hold your index fingers up in front of you with the tip of one touching the tip of the other. They should be about 5 inches (12 cm) away from your eyes.

2. Now focus your eyes on something on the other side of the room. You should see a sausage shape "appear" between your two fingers. Again, each eye is seeing things from a slightly different angle. When your brain puts the images together, your fingers seem to overlap to make the sausage.

III. My Friend, the Cyclops

If you've read any Greek myths, you may know about the cyclops— a giant with one eye in the middle of his forehead. How would your best friend look as a cyclops?

What to Do:
1. Put your forehead and your nose against a friend's forehead and nose.

2. Look straight ahead as if you were looking at something on the other side of the room. What has happened to your friend's eyes?

Amazing Animation

Animated cartoons are made from a series of drawings. Each one is just a *little* changed from the one before it. When they run by your eyes quickly, you see them "move." Try making your own animated drawings — it's easy.

What You Need:
some lightweight typewriter paper 8½ x 11 inches (21 cm x 27.5 cm)
scissors
a pencil
a crayon, marker pen or colored pencil for drawing
tape

What to Do:

1. Fold your paper crosswise into four equal strips. Cut the paper along the foldlines. You now have four strips.

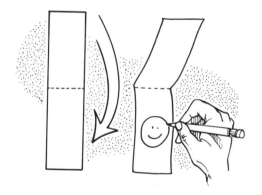

2. Take one strip and fold it in half. Then open it out flat. On the bottom half make a simple drawing. Why not start with a happy face?

3. Now fold the paper so that it covers your drawing. Your drawing should show through. (If you can't see it very well, hold your folded paper against a window.)

4. Trace your drawing onto the top flap—but make a little change in it. Perhaps your happy face is now wearing a frown.

5. Take a pencil and lay it on the edge of the top flap. Tape the edge of the paper to the pencil with a small piece of tape. Roll the paper onto the pencil, up to the fold.

6. Hold the back flap against a desk or table. Roll the pencil up and down so that the top drawing appears and disappears. When you go fast enough, you'll see an animated face that keeps changing from happy to sad.

7. Try some other animated drawings — maybe a winking eye, or a bird that flies. Try some in color — maybe a traffic light that goes from red to green. The drawings that work best are the ones that change just a little bit.

What's a Thaumatrope?

Your eyes hold onto the image of something for a split second after the thing is out of sight. A thaumatrope is a toy that uses this trick of the eye. (Toys like this gave people the idea of how to make movies.)

What You Need:

a piece of heavy paper or light cardboard, 2 inches (5 cm)
    square (light paper won't work well)
a pen or colored marker
a pencil with an eraser
a thumbtack or pushpin
a pen

What to Do:

1. Turn the square of paper so that one corner is toward you. Draw a fish bowl in the center of the paper.

2. Turn the paper over to the other side. Draw a fish in the center of the page. (If you hold your paper against a window, the bowl will show through to help you place the fish.)

3. Use the thumbtack to stick the paper to the pencil's eraser. (See the drawing.)

4. Hold the pencil upright between your palms. Roll the pencil back and forth so that the paper flips from one side to the other. As you roll the pencil faster and faster, you'll see the fish *in* the bowl.

Spooky Trees

See a strange leafless tree — and find out about the inside of your eye.

What You Need:
a flashlight
a dark room with a blank wall

What to Do:

1. Close one eye. Cover it with your hand.

2. With your other eye, stare at a blank wall in a darkened room. At the same time, shine the flashlight toward the outer edge of the open eye. Don't stare straight at the flashlight, or you'll be so dazzled that you won't see anything!

3. After a minute or so, you'll see a big branching tree on the wall. This "tree" is the image of the blood vessels at the back of your eye. (You may have to try the flashlight at different distances from your eye, to find the right place. About 1 foot (30 cm) away worked for me.)

Red Eye Specials

You open the package of photos taken at your birthday party and — eeuuw! gross! — all your friends look like red-eyed monsters! What happened? Whoever took the pictures aimed the flash right at your friends' eyes. Eyeballs contain lots of red blood vessels. The light from the flashbulbs went into their eyes and bounced back to the camera. So the picture shows the blood vessels! If you'd rather not have a picture of the *inside* of your friends' eyes, have them look a little away from the flash. Or get an extension that puts the flash higher up, so that the light doesn't go into their eyes.

Giant Eyes

If you came face-to-face with the world's biggest eyes, what would you be looking at? A few scared fishermen have actually found out, when giant squids wrapped themselves around their boats. Giant squids can have eyeballs about 8 inches (well over 200 mm) in diameter. That's about twice as large as the eyes of the world's largest animal, the great blue whale. And it's about *10 times* as large as your eyes.

More About Colors and Light

Have you ever watched a black and white program on TV? Did you wish you could see it in color? Wouldn't it be dull if we saw *everything* in black and white? We'd never know the beauty of green grass and blue sky. Lots of animals — including dogs and cats — can't see many colors, so we're very lucky that we can.

On the inside of your eye, at the back, is the *retina*. The retina is made up of about 130 million cells that are sensitive to light. These cells are joined to nerves that send sight messages to your brain. There are two main kinds of retina cells. They are named for their shapes: *cones* and *rods*.

Cones let you see in color. They are grouped toward the center of the retina. This means that you see the color of something better when you look right at it. Some cones see only red light, some see only blue light, and some see only green light. These cones can work together in different ways. For instance, if both red and blue cones are at work, you can see a bluish-red color called magenta. And if all the colors of light come into your eye at once, can you guess what you see? It's hard to believe at first, but you see *white* light.

Here's a very interesting thing about light. Light that looks white to you really has all the colors of the rainbow in it. You can split white light into its separate colors with a piece of glass or with water. (See page 54.) The complete range of rainbow colors is called the *spectrum*.

Does this mean that you can make white paint by mixing together all the colors in your paintbox? No — you'll get something closer to black. It's confusing, but mixing colors of light is not the same thing as mixing colors of paint.

When you paint a picture of a green apple, it looks green because the paint is letting green light escape from it. It is absorbing (taking in) all the other colors of light. In a funny way, the green apple you painted has every color *but* green in it! A blob of all your paints mixed together will hardly let any light escape. So it will look almost black.

Cones, like many other sense receptors, can get fatigued (tired out). If you stare at the green apple for a minute or so, your green cones will stop sending messages. If you close your eyes or look at a white sheet of paper, you'll see a red *after-image* of the apple for a few seconds. Your red cones have taken over while the green ones have a short rest.

Have you every heard of people who are color blind? Color blind people can see as clearly as anyone else. But some of their color cones don't work properly. Usually, they can see some colors but can't tell red and green apart. It's not a very serious problem — they just have to be careful about reading traffic lights! (The red light is the one at the top.)

Cones work well in bright light. In dim light, we use our rods instead. Rods can only see in black and white. That is why, in a dark room, we can see the outlines of things, but not their colors.

Have you noticed that when you first turn out your bedroom light, the room seems very black? After a while, though, the room seems to get brighter. It isn't the room that's changing, it's your eyes. First your pupils open wide to let in more light. Then your dim-light rods start to work, while your bright-light cones go off duty.

With cones and rods, it's almost as if your eyes give you two senses of sight instead of one!

AMANZING FACT

Neat Night Trick

Here's a trick that lets you see something more clearly when it's very dark. Look a little to the side of the thing, instead of right at it. When there's not much light, you use your rods to see. There are more rods at the sides of your retina than in the center. If you look to the side, you're focusing the dim light where your eyes can see it best.

In a Spin

When several colors of the spectrum reach your eyes at once, you see them in a different way.

What You Need:
cardboard
white drawing paper
a drinking glass
scissors
pencil
glue
paints or colored markers
2 pieces of string, each about
    3 feet (1 m) long

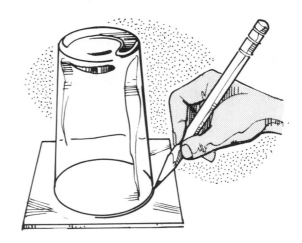

What to Do:

1. Use the glass to trace two circles on a piece of cardboard. Cut out the disks of cardboard.

2. Use the same glass to trace two circles on paper. Cut them out.

3. Take one circle of paper and fold it in half. Then fold this half circle in half to get a quarter circle. Fold it again. Open out the paper circle and make it flat.

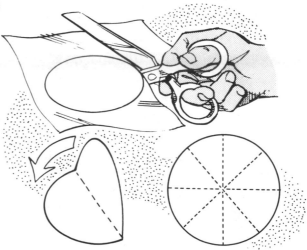

4. Glue the circle onto a cardboard disk.

5. You can still see all the fold lines on the piece of paper, making eight sectors (pie-shaped pieces). Paint one sector red, the next one green, the next one red, and so on around the circle.

6. All the fold lines cross at the center of the disk. Mark two dots near the center of the disk. The dots must be an equal distance from the center, or the disk won't spin properly. (*See drawing 1*.) Leave enough space between the dots (½ inch [1 cm] or more) so that the space in between won't tear. Use a sharp pencil point or a nail to make holes through these dots.

7. Thread a piece of string through one hole and back through the other. (*See drawing 2*.) Knot the string.

DRAWING 1.

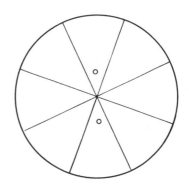

DRAWING 2.

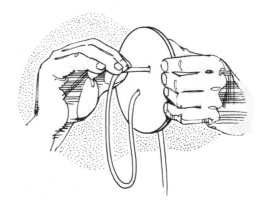

8. Move the disk along until it is in the middle of the string loop.

9. Put a finger through each end of the loop. (*See drawing 3.*) Twirl the disk until the string is very twisted.

10. Pull the string tight by pulling your fingers apart. The disk will spin. If you keep letting your fingers go closer together and then pulling them apart, the disk will keep spinning. How do the green and red sections look when they are spinning?

11. Divide the second paper circle into six equal sectors, as shown in drawing 4. Now color the sectors the six colors of the spectrum. (*See drawing 4.*)

12. Glue the circle to the cardboard disk, make the holes, and thread the string, just as you did with the red-green disk.

13. Make the disk spin. What do you see? (If you had pure colors, just as they are in the spectrum, you would see white. But you may actually see a sort of dirty gray.)

DRAWING 3.

DRAWING 4.

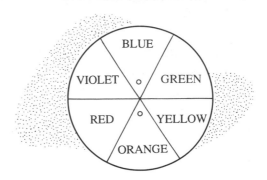

Make Your Own Rainbow

Use water to split white light into all the colors of the spectrum.

What You Need:
a clear glass bowl
a small mirror
a drinking glass
water
a piece of white paper
a sunny day

What to Do:

1. Fill a clear glass bowl with water. Set it in a sunny place.

2. Put a small mirror in the water, facing the sun. Tilt the mirror at an angle. Keep an eye on the ceiling.

3. When you get the angle right, a rainbow of colors will appear on the ceiling!

or

1. Pour water into a clear drinking glass.

2. Sit the glass on a sunny windowsill. Or hold it up to the sunlight.

3. Move the glass around. Soon you'll see rainbow patterns on the ceiling or the floor. If you put a white piece of paper on the floor, the rainbow pattern will show up more clearly.

Colorful After-Images

If your eyes get tired of looking at one color, they will come up with another one!

What You Need:
several sheets of white drawing paper
poster paints or colored markers

What to Do:

1. On a piece of white drawing paper draw a big apple. Color the apple a nice bright *green*.

2. Put your drawing next to a blank white sheet of paper. Stare at your drawing for at least a minute. Try not to move your eyes.

3. Now look at the blank sheet of paper. What do you see?

4. Each color of the spectrum has an "after-image" color. Find out what they are. Take some smaller sheets of paper. On each one make a big dot of color: red, violet, blue, yellow and orange. Stare at each dot for a minute or so. Then look at a blank sheet of paper. Let a friend try this too. Are your friend's after-image colors the same as yours?

Phantom Colors

Can black and white ever look like color? Try this project and see.

What You Need:
cardboard paper plate
scissors
compass and pencil
thick-tip black marker **or** black poster paint and brush
pencil with sharpened end
a bit of soft modelling clay, Silly Putty or even bubble gum

What to Do:

1. If the paper plate has a stiff, turned-up rim, carefully cut it off.

2. Use the compass and pencil to copy the design on this page onto the paper plate. If you don't know how to use a compass yet, ask an older brother or sister or your parents to help you.

3. Color the design as shown. The black parts have to be very black. (Grayish watercolor black or lead pencil black won't do.)

4. Push the pencil through the center of the disk, sharpened point down. The design on the disk should be face up.

5. Spin the disk like a top. Again, if you're not sure how to do this, ask an older person for help.

6. If you find that the pencil is slipping through the hole you made, do this. Cover the hole with a thin little piece of clay, putty or even chewed up bubble gum. Then push the pencil through again.

7. When the disk is spinning fast, you will see bars and flashes of colors. What colors do you see? Do other people see the same ones?

The colors you see are after-images. In the 1950s, everyone had black and white TV. A TV show host spun a wheel like this on his program. People watching at home were thrilled to see flashes of color (made by their eyes, not their black and white TV sets).

Find Your Blind Spot

Every person has a "blind spot" at the back of each eye. This is the place where the optic nerve leaves the eye. It has no rods and cones. We can't see any small image that falls on this spot. Usually this doesn't matter, because we look at things with two eyes. To find your blind spot, do this. Hold this book in both hands, with your arms stretched out in front of you. Shut your *left* eye. Stare at the circle with your *right* eye. Slowly move the book toward you. At some point, the cross will disappear. Its image has fallen on the blind spot of your right eye. When you open your left eye, the cross will pop back into view.

What Bees See

Bees, like people, see in color. However, they are "tuned in" to different parts of the spectrum than we are. Bees can't see red. They can see ultraviolet light, though, which people are blind to. A flower that looks white to us may have stripes on it that bees' eyes can see. These secret markings act like runways to help the bee make a safe landing. They also point to the center of the flower, where the bee will find sweet nectar.

How Do You Hear?

Do you know where the tiniest bones in your body are? They're not in your fingers or toes, as you might expect. They're in your ears!

Your ears have a lot more parts than you can see on the outside. Usually, when you talk about your ears, you mean the flaps on the sides of your head. But those flaps, whose proper name is *pinnae*, are just sound collectors. Try cupping your hand around your ear while you are listening to something. You'll make a larger sound collector and hear the sound more clearly.

Many animals have bigger and better sound collectors than we do. Think of the tall pinnae that rabbits have. An elephant can have pinnae 3 feet (1 m) wide. Try standing beside your cat or dog when it's having a nap. Snap your fingers. You can see your pet's pinnae turn to pick up the sound. We can't do that with our ears—although some people can wiggle them a little!

The inside of your ear is like the maze in a fantasy game. It has rooms with guarded entryways. It takes many surprising twists and turns. The maze begins with your *ear canal*. This is a curved tube about 1 inch (3 cm) long. The ear canal has some bristly hairs and sticky ear wax to trap dirt and stop insects from getting any farther. It leads to your *middle* ear.

Stretched tight across the entrance to the middle ear is your *eardrum*. It is a thin piece of skin that vibrates (shakes) when sound reaches it. Behind the eardrum is an open space filled with air. Running like a bridge across this space are three tiny bones joined together. They're named for their shapes: the *hammer*, the *anvil* and the *stirrup*. These bones amplify (make louder) the vibrations that reach the eardrum. The last bone in line touches the *oval window*. This is another thin piece of skin like the eardrum. It covers the entrance to the *inner ear*.

Inside the inner ear is a twisty tube called the *cochlea*. Cochlea is the Greek word for "snail," and that's just what the tube looks like. The cochlea is filled with liquid. It is also lined with thousands of tiny hairs. These hairs wave back and forth as sound vibrations make the liquid move.

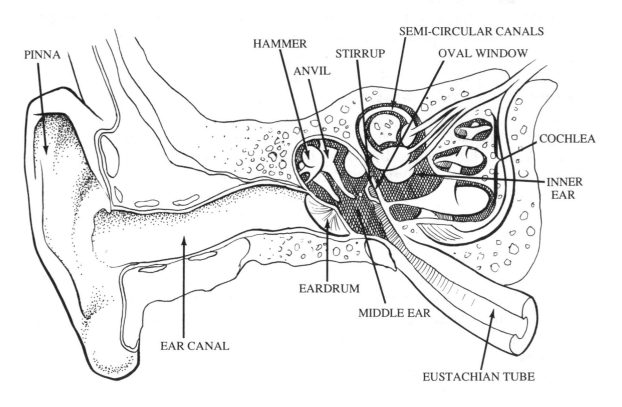

The hairs are connected to nerves. The nerves carry the sound message into your brain, which lets you "hear" the sound. The whole twisting, turning journey through the maze happens in an instant. And it lets you enjoy music, the wind through the trees, or your mother's voice.

If you take good care of your ears, all of those tiny amazing parts can keep working for you. Never poke anything in your ear. It could get stuck in your ear. Or you could make a hole in your eardrum so that it can't vibrate properly. Blow your nose gently, especially when you have a cold. Your nose and your middle ears are joined by tubes. If you blow your nose too hard, you can push germs into your middle ears. If your ears ever hurt or buzz, go to the doctor.

One final point about ears. Did you ever wonder why you have two instead of one? To hold up your glasses? Nope. A sound coming from off to the left is louder in your left ear than in your right ear. This means that you can tell what direction the sound is coming from. For instance, when you hear your sister shout your name, you know which way to turn to see her. This is a skill we don't usually think about, but it comes in handy every day.

AMAZING FACT

When Krakatoa Cracked Open

What was the biggest bang since people have been keeping written records of what they heard? It was probably the eruption of Krakatoa, a volcanic island in Indonesia, in 1883. The explosion was 26 times as powerful as the largest hydrogen bomb ever tested. Rocks from the explosion were hurled 34 miles (55 km) into the air. Dust travelled 3,313 miles (5330 km). And the noise? The sound of the eruption was heard like "the roar of heavy guns" on an island 2,968 miles (4776 km) away from Krakatoa. Altogether, people on about one-thirteenth of the earth's surface heard Krakatoa splitting apart.

Great-Grandma's Gramophone

Over 60 years ago, record players had big horns to make the music loud enough to hear. You can use a needle and a cone of paper to hear a record the old-fashioned way.

What You Need:
a piece of construction paper or other heavy paper,
    about 18 inches (45 cm) square
tape
a fine sewing needle
and old record (make *sure* it's one that nobody wants any more,
    because this activity will scratch it)

What to Do:
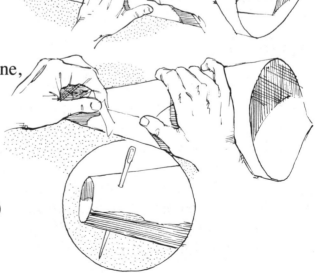
1. Starting at one corner, roll the paper into a wide-ended cone. Tape the outside edge of the paper to hold it in place.

2. Push a needle through the cone, about ½ inch (2 cm) from the small end.

3. Put the record on a record player's turntable. (If you're using the family stereo, ask permission before doing this.) Turn the record player on, so that the record is spinning around.

4. Touch the end of the needle to a groove in the record. Keep your hand as still as you can. Inside the groove are many tiny "teeth." As the needle catches in them, it vibrates. The paper cone amplifies these vibrations (makes them louder) so that you can hear them. You should be able to hear some words and music—although maybe not very clearly.

The early record players were *not* powered by electricity. You had to turn a handle on the side to make the turntable go around. After a while, the turntable would start to slow down and the record would sound very funny.

Hear There and Everywhere

Prove that two ears are better than one. It's hard to figure out where a sound is coming from with one ear blocked.

What You Need:
ear plugs or cotton balls
a clock with a loud ticking sound
a chair
a blindfold
a partner

What to Do:

1. Gently block your ears with earplugs or with cotton. Make sure that you can't hear hear the loudly ticking clock.

2. Wait outside while your partner hides the clock somewhere in a room. Have your partner blindfold you and lead you to a chair in the center of the room.

3. Remove the plug from *one* ear.

4. Try to point to the direction you think the tick is coming from. Is it harder than you thought it would be?

5. With your blindfold on, go on a search for the clock. (Your partner should stay close to you and keep you from bumping into things.) Is it easier to figure out the direction of the clock when you are moving, or when you are sitting still?

Bone Tones

Sound can travel through the bones in your head, right up to your inner ears.

What You Need:
a metal saucepan
a big all-metal serving fork (a table fork will work too, but the sound won't be very loud)

What to Do:

1. Strike the prongs of the fork against the metal saucepan. It will make a loud ringing sound.

2. Hold the fork next to your ear. Wait until the sound has *almost* faded away.

3. Right away, put the handle of the fork between your teeth. What happens? What does this tell you about how you hear your own voice?

Oven Rack Chimes
You'll be amazed by what you hear !

What You Need:
a metal oven rack
2 pieces of strong string,
   each about 20 inches (50 cm) long
a wooden spoon
a partner

What to Do:

1. Knot the string around the top bar of the oven rack, one string at each corner. (*See the drawing.*)

2. Wrap the other ends of the strings around your index fingers several times. Now the oven rack can hang from your fingers.

3. Stick your index fingers in your ears. Lean forward so that the oven rack is hanging free. It must not be touching anything.

rack. You'll be surprised! How do you think the sound reached your ears?

4. Ask your partner to run the wooden spoon along the oven

5. Trade places and let your partner hear the chimes.

Thunderstorm Countdown

You're lying in bed on a summer night. A bright flash of lightning wakes you up. Then — ka-boom! a big clap of thunder makes you sit right up in bed. Thunderstorms are exciting, but sometimes a little scary too. Would you feel better if you knew how far away the lightning struck?

The lightning made that big loud noise as it cut through the air. The flash reached you much sooner than the thunder did, though. This is because light travels much faster than sound. You can use this fact to figure out how far away the lightning is.

As soon as you see the lightning flash, start counting the seconds like this: *one*-thousand, *two*-thousand, *three*-thousand . . . Stop when you hear the thunder. Sound takes about 5 seconds to travel 1 mile (3 seconds to travel 1 km). So if you counted to 15, it means the lightning struck about 3 miles (5 km) away from you. By counting a few thunderclaps like this, you can even find out if the storm is getting closer or moving away. All this counting can make you very drowsy. Before you know it, you'll be back to sleep.

More about Sounds

Look up from this book and listen ...

What did you hear? If you're at home, you might have heard your dad's voice in the kitchen, the radio or TV in the living room, and a car going by in the street. You can't close your ears to shut out sound the way you can close your eyes. Instead, the hearing part of your brain decides what you need to hear. While you were reading, you probably didn't notice the sounds around you.

Your brain also lets you pick out one sound to listen to. Try it. First, you might pay attention to a song on the radio. Then, without moving, you can shut out the radio and listen to what your dad is saying. Your ears didn't change in any way. Your brain lets you switch from one sound to another.

All sounds are made by something vibrating (shaking back and forth very fast). These vibrations make whatever is around the thing vibrate too. Sound vibrations, called *sound waves,* can travel through air, through water, and through solid things. When the vibrations reach our ears, we hear the sound.

Most sounds reach us through the air. Our friends' voices come to us this way. We hear the sound made when their vocal cords vibrate. You can feel your own vocal cords vibrate. Just put your hand to your throat while you say something.

Did you know that you can't hear your voice the same way other people can? It sounds richer and deeper to you than it does to them. This is because you hear your own voice not just through the air, but through the bones in your head. If you want a better idea of how you sound to everybody else, listen to your tape-recorded voice. You'll be surprised!

Sounds can be very *high-pitched*, like the top note of a piano, or *low-pitched*, like the bottom note. The faster a thing vibrates, the higher the sound it makes. If you have a two-speed record player, you can prove this for yourself. When you play a record, the needle vibrates in the grooves. Play a $33^1/_3$ record at 45 speed. The record will go around faster and the singers' voices will sound pretty squeaky.

We use Hertz (Hz) to describe how fast a sound wave vibrates. If it vibrates 500 times a second, it has a measurement of 500 Hz. People can hear sounds from about 30 Hz (a *very* low rumble) to about 20,000 Hz (a *very* high squeak). Sounds higher than 20,000 Hz are called *ultrasound*. Many animals can hear ultrasound. Some people call their dogs by blowing on a "dog whistle" which human ears can't hear.

Sounds can be loud or soft. The loudness of sounds is measured in decibels (dB). A whisper has a loudness of about 20 dB. You talk to your friends at about 60 dB. Sounds over 100 dB make you want to cover your ears and get away. 140 dB is a painful blast of sound, like a jet plane taking off close by.

Loud noises can make the tiny parts inside your ear vibrate too much. This can cause deafness. Never shout into someone's ear. Keep the sound turned down if you wear headphones to listen to music. A loud music concert can make your ears ring for hours afterward. That's a sign that the loud sound was damaging your ears. Many musicians have lost some of their hearing from blasting their eardrums with too-loud music. Think of all the beautiful sounds you can hear now — the laughter of people you love, music, bird songs. Take care of your ears so that you'll go on hearing with them.

See Some Sounds

With a "soundscope," you can actually see some sound waves jiggling on the wall.

What You Need:
a coffee can or a large soup can, with both ends removed
a big balloon
scissors
a small mirror
a strong elastic band
white glue

What to Do:

1. First you need to stretch the balloon. Blow it up and tie the end. Leave the balloon for a couple of hours.

2. Untie the balloon to let the air out. If you can't untie it, cut the end off with scissors. (Don't *prick* the balloon — it may tear into many small pieces.)

3. With scissors, cut a circle out of the balloon. The circle must be big enough to stretch over one end of the can. (Place the end of the can on the balloon before

you cut. That way, you can see how big a circle you need.)

4. Ask someone to stretch the balloon piece over the end of the can. Put an elastic band over the end of the can to hold the balloon in place. The balloon should be as smooth and tightly stretched as a drumskin.

5. You need a very tiny mirror, about ½ inch (1 cm) square. If you cannot find a mirror this small in a hobby or toy store, ask an adult to break a small pocket mirror for you. Here's a safe way to do it. Wrap the mirror in several thicknesses of paper towel. Fold over the ends so no glass can escape. Hit the mirror once or twice with a hammer. Unwrap carefully, and choose a small piece of mirror about ½ inch (1 cm) square. Be very careful not to cut yourself. Rewrap the rest of the glass and throw it in the garbage.

6. Glue the piece of mirror to the center of the balloon, shiny side out.

7. Now you need a bright sunny day. Stand near a window with sun streaming through it. Move the soundscope until the mirror catches the sunlight and reflects a spot of light onto the wall.

8. Sing or shout into the open end of the can. The sound waves you make will make the balloon vibrate (shake very fast). The vibrations will be reflected on the wall, so that you can see them.

9. Try making low sounds and high sounds, loud sounds and soft sounds. How do the patterns on the wall change?

Tick Tricks

Use a watch to find out some interesting things about the way sound travels.

What You Need:
a ticking watch
two soup bowls or salad bowls
a long wooden table or wooden
    railing of a staircase

What to Do:
1. Sit at a table with one bowl in front of you. Hold the other soup bowl against your ear.

2. Hold the ticking watch just inside the soup bowl on the table.

3. Move your head so that the bowl against your ear is right over the bowl on the table. Where do you hear the ticking now? The soup bowl on the table collected the sound waves from the watch. It sent them up to the other bowl as an echo.

4. Now try something else. Put the ticking watch on one end of a long wooden table. (Or set the watch on the post at the top of a long wooden stair railing.) Press your ear against the other end of the table (or railing). What do you hear ? Sound waves can travel through solid things as well as through the air.

Echolocation

For bats, ears take the place of eyes! Even on the blackest nights, bats can find food and keep from bumping into things. How do they do it? They make very high-pitched sounds and listen for the echo. This is called *echolocation.* Bats can tell how far ahead a thing is by how long the echo takes to return. They can also tell the size and shape of the thing by changes in the way the sound bounces back. Dolphins and whales use echolocation too, to make their way through vast oceans.

Good Vibrations

All musical instruments have parts that vibrate. You can make some simple vibrating soundmakers of your own. The first is very easy. The second one is more work — but it makes a more interesting sound, too.

I. Instant Whistle

What You Need:

an empty box from coughdrops or square pieces of gum

What to Do:

1. Tear off the cardboard flaps at one end of the box.

2. Put the open end of the of the box to your lips. Blow. What happens? Can you see the box vibrating?

II. Drinking Straw Flute

What You Need:

at least 5 big *thin* plastic drinking
    straws (the kind restaurants use
    for milkshakes)
a ruler
scissors
tape
a clean, empty tin can

What to Do:

1. Measure 1 inch (3 cm) at the end of a straw. Rub the edge of the ruler back and forth against the end of the straw to flatten it.

2. Cut off both corners at an angle, starting about ½ inch (1 cm) from the end. (*See drawing 1.*)

DRAWING 1.

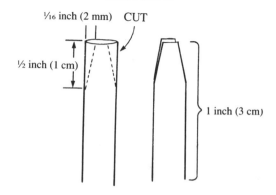

3. Put the flattened end in your mouth. Push it in far enough that your lips don't touch the flattened part. It has to be free to vibrate. Blow hard. If no sound comes out, try flattening the end again. (You may have to flatten and cut several straws before you get this right.)

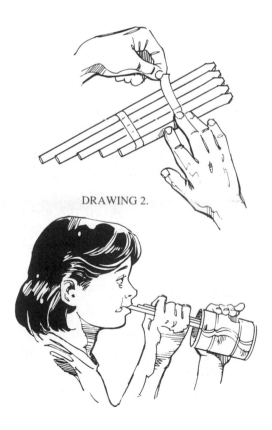

DRAWING 2.

4. When you are happy with the sound the first straw makes, cut a second one. Cut ¾ inch (2 cm) off the end of the second straw. Then flatten and cut the end as you did on the first straw.

5. Blow into the second straw. Is its sound higher or lower than the first straw?

6. Cut 1½ inches (4 cm) off the third straw, 2¼ inches (6 cm) off the fourth straw, and 3 inches (8 cm) off the fifth straw. Flatten and cut the end of each straw.

7. Tape all the straws together. (*See drawing 2.*) Now you can play them all at once. If you blow your flute into a tin can, the air in the can will vibrate too. This will make the sound louder.

Secret Messages

You can whisper a secret message — and a long piece of string will carry your words right to your friend's ear.

What You Need:
2 clean, empty 12½ ounce (355 mL)
    juice cans
a nail
a hammer
a piece of string about 20 feet
    (6 m) long

What to Do:

1. First you need to make a hole in the bottom of each can. Ask permission *before* using the hammer and nail. Hold the nail with its point against the center of the metal bottom. Tap the head of the nail lightly with a hammer. After about four or five taps, the nail will go through the metal.

2. Push one end of the string through the hole. Pull the string out through the open end of the can. Tie a big fat knot in it. (Knot it several times in one place if you need to. You don't want the knot to slip through the hole you made.) Let the string slide back through the can so that just the knot is holding it.

3. Take the other end of the string and thread it through the other can. Tie a knot in the end.

4. Hand one can to a friend. You and your friend should walk apart from each other until the string is pulled tight. (You can do this outdoors or indoors.) The string must be held very

straight, and it must not touch anything.

5. Take turns. One person whispers into one can, while the other listens with a can held to one ear. You will find that you can hear very soft whispers. Your voices are making the string vibrate.

Super Squeakers

What's as loud as a jackhammer — but we can't hear it? The answer is: a baby mouse! Rats, mice, hamsters and other small rodents love to chatter among themselves. Most of their sounds are so high-pitched — 70,000 to 140,000 Hertz — that human ears can't hear them. (To "eavesdrop" on rodents, people have to use special electronic instruments.) If a baby mouse is frightened, it can squeak *very* loudly. We can't hear the baby's 100 decibel fussing, but its mother certainly can.

Loudness in the Lab

The loudest noise ever made by people was created in an American laboratory in 1965. A steel and concrete horn blasted out 210 decibels of noise. A sound this loud can drill a hole through the side of your house!

Some Other Senses—and ESP

As you've read through this book, you've learned a lot about your senses. You already know that there are more than five of them. In fact, your skin alone has more than five kinds of sense receptors.

Your ears, too, give you more than one sense. They're not just for hearing. They also control your sense of balance. Inside your inner ear, near your cochlea, are three curved tubes. They're called the *semicircular canals*. Like the cochlea, they're filled with liquid, and have waving hairs attached to nerves. The liquid moves when you turn your head. The nerves send a message to your brain so that it can keep track of how you're moving. If you spin too fast, the liquid in the canals really sloshes around. Even when you stop spinning, the liquid keeps moving for a short while. This is why you feel like you're still twirling.

When you are just standing still, two other inner ear organs help you balance. They're little sacs called the *saccule* and the *utricle*. They're joined to the semicircular canals and have the same liquid in them. They report when your body is going off balance. Then your brain sends a message to your muscles to get you back in balance. Even when you are trying to stand very still, your muscles will always be making little shifts to keep you balanced.

You have lots of other senses. Every joint in your body has sensors sending messages to your brain. Because of them, you always know, without looking, if your arm is bent or straight. You know where your feet are. Wouldn't it be a weird feeling if you had to look to find out?

Sensors in your stomach tell your brain whether your stomach is empty or full. If it's empty, you feel hungry and you eat. Other sensors tell your brain when your body is low on water. You feel thirsty and have a drink. Another sense is still a bit mysterious. We — and many other animals — seem to have a sense of time. Even without clocks, we can keep to a regular pattern of sleeping and waking.

ESP stands for *extra-sensory perception*. This means finding out things without using your senses. Many different kinds of ESP have been described. For example, *telepathy* means being able to send a "thought message" to another person. *Precognition* means knowing something will happen before it does.

People sometimes ask me if I believe in ESP. I have to answer this way. I believe many things happen to us that we don't yet understand. But there is still a lot that we don't know about how our senses work. As we learn more, we may find out that these mysterious happenings aren't beyond our senses after all. We are probably sensing a lot more than we think we are. Dogs can "smell fear" — the special smell that sweat has when we're frightened. Perhaps people can, too.

Here's another thing. Our pupils get a little smaller when we look at something we don't like. They get bigger when we like what we're seeing. This is not something we can control. It seems that people see each other's eyes doing this. Some people were shown a photo of a woman with small pupils. They said she looked unfriendly. Then they were shown another photo. It was just like the first, except that the woman's pupils were wider. The people said that she looked friendly in this one. But they were not able to say what had struck them as different about the two pictures!

Perhaps when we get strange "feelings" about other people, we're really just using our senses.

How Dizzy Can You Get?

You already know that spinning around like a top can make you dizzy. Here's something that's even better — or worse, depending on how you look at it!

What You Need:

a yardstick or meter stick

What to Do:

1. Hold the stick with one end on the floor. Put your forehead against the other end. Keeping your head against the end, walk around the stick three or four times. Try to keep the stick upright and in one place.

2. Stand up. Now sit down somewhere and wait for the room to stop going around!

Try Some Telepathy

Is it possible for you to receive a thought message from a friend? Try it and see.

What You Need

a deck of playing cards
a table and chairs
a pile of books or a box
paper and pencil
a blindfold
a partner

What to Do:

1. Remove the jokers, so that your deck has 52 cards. Shuffle the cards.

2. Sit across from your friend at a table. Put some books or a box in the middle of the table so that your side of the table is hidden from your friend.

3. Put the deck of cards face down in front of you. Ask your friend to close his or her eyes. Pick up a card from the deck and stare hard at it, concentrating on its color. Tell your friend to try hard to pick up a message from you about the card's color.

4. Ask your friend whether the card is red or black. When your friend answers, don't tell whether the answer is wrong or right. Keep track on a piece of paper, though. Keep going through the deck, until all the cards are used up.

5. Add up your friend's score.

Something about Chance:

There are equal numbers of red and black cards in the deck. Each time you turn over a card, your friend has one chance in two of getting it right. Therefore, just by chance, you would expect your friend to be right about half the time. This means your friend would get about 26 right answers. If you run through the deck a few times, your friend may score as high as 30 on one run, and as low as 22 on another. But after a lot of runs, the average score will be about 26 right answers. If after many runs, you have an average quite a bit higher than 26, you might be more sensitive in some way than most people. The people who study this ability call it ESP, since we still have no idea what senses might be involved in sending a "thought message."

Two Senses' Worth

Do you need your eyes, as well as your ears, to keep your balance?

What You Need:
chalk
binoculars

What to Do:

1. Draw a chalk line on the sidewalk or on a concrete basement floor. (Before drawing on the floor, ask permission.)

2. Put the binoculars to your eyes the wrong way around. The floor and your feet should look *very* far away.

3. Now, looking through the binoculars, walk along the chalk line. Is it hard to stay on the line?

4. Put away the binoculars and try something else. Stand on one foot. How long can you balance? Time yourself with the second hand of a watch or by counting: *one*-thousand, *two*-thousand.

5. Now try balancing on one foot with your eyes closed. Time yourself. How did you do without the help of your eyes?

Synesthesia—Strange and Rare

There are a few people in the world who "see" sounds or smells. Their senses are mixed together in a way that the rest of us can hardly imagine. This mixing of senses is called *synesthesia*. One synesthetic woman said that she was forever mixing up the names of two friends. The reason? Both names were green. And she really meant that she saw the color green when she heard those names. Another man saw tastes as shapes. He once said that his chicken dinner had too many corners on it. People with synesthesia enjoy the extra richness of their senses. But sometimes they find it hard to explain them to other people!

Snakes with an Extra Sense

A rattlesnake can "see" the body heat given off by other animals, just as clearly as we can see colors. It has special heat-sensing pits just under its eyes. The snake's eyes and these pits work together to give it a "heat picture" of living things nearby. Even on the darkest night, the rattlesnake can find its prey and strike.

Can You Find Your Own Nose ?

Close your eyes. Stretch out your arm in front of you. Point your index finger (the one next to your thumb). Bend your elbow and turn your finger back toward your face. Touch the tip of your nose. (No peeking!)

How did you do?

Try again. Close your eyes. Stretch your arm out to the side. Point your finger. Bend your elbow and turn your finger back toward your head. Touch your earlobe. We have a pretty good idea of where our body parts are in space, but we can make mistakes, too!

Inventions to Stretch Our Senses

Our senses give us exciting links with the world around us. But it is also true that anything we can sense, some other creature can sense better. Suppose, for instance, that you take your dog for a walk. You might smell a flowering plant or someone's dinner cooking while you walk. On the same walk, your dog might enjoy *hundreds* of different scents—and not just recent ones, but smells that have lingered for days.

We can do something, though, that other animals can't do. We can use our brains to invent things that extend our senses. In this way, we can make our senses more powerful than those of any other animal.

Eyeglasses, telescopes and microscopes have been around for hundreds of years. Today, we have telescopes that can see to the edge of the known universe, 5 billion light years away. (A light year is the distance light can travel in one year. This is an immensely long way, since light can travel about 180,000 miles [300,000 km] in a *second*.) We have microscopes that let us see inside our own body cells. Some microscopes can make things look 100,000 times bigger than they really are.

We've had cameras to take still pictures for about 150 years. Nowadays, we also have movie and television cameras. They let us see moving pictures with color and sound. Cameras are like our eyes in many ways. They don't focus or react to light as smoothly as our eyes do, though. And no film can "see" colors as well as our eyes can. However, cameras do magical things for us. They let us travel through space and time. We can watch a live broadcast showing astronauts in space. Later, we can watch an old movie of the first airplanes trying to take off, over 80 years ago.

Television cameras act as our eyes in places where human beings can't go. Cameras have plunged deep into the ocean to photograph sunken treasure ships. Cameras on the *Voyager 2* spacecraft have sent back pictures from the planet Uranus, more than 1 billion miles (1.5 billion km) from Earth. Cameras circling the Earth on weather satellites warn us of hurricanes.

We can take pictures of infrared light, which our eyes can't see directly. Sick plants give off less infrared than healthy ones. An infrared picture, taken from a plane, can show which forests are dying. X-rays can go right through our flesh to the bones underneath. Doctors use x-ray pictures to find out if you have broken your arm.

We've been able to extend our other senses, too. Radios and telephones let us hear voices on the other side of the world. Records, audio tapes and compact disks let us enjoy our favorite songs over and over. A hundred years ago, you could only hear singers you liked if you went to their concerts. And most people could not afford to buy the tickets.

We have found many uses for ultrasound, the high-pitched sounds our ears can't hear by themselves. Copying bats and dolphins, ships and submarines use sonar for echolocation. Special machines change the ultrasound echos into a sound we can hear. Ultrasound is also used to check babies before they are born, while they are still inside their mother's abdomens.

All these amazing inventions might make you feel that your own human senses don't amount to much. But this isn't true. We can invent things to make life easier for blind or deaf people. But we haven't yet invented anything that replaces an eye. We can't bring back normal hearing to someone who is deaf.

Most sense-stretching inventions don't mean much if you haven't got your own wonderful sense organs. What good is a photograph if you can't see? What good is a record if you can't hear? Take good care of your sense organs so that your life can always be a sense adventure.

Thrilling Sound Effects

Before television came along, people listened to adventure stories on the radio — and *imagined* how the scenes looked. You can use a tape recorder to create your own exciting program with sound effects.

What You Need:

a tape recorder and microphone (if you don't have a tape recorder at home, perhaps one of your friends does — or there might be one at school that you could use)

Sound Effects Supplies:

(a) rain — ¼ cup (50 mL) dried peas and a metal cake pan.
   Shake the pan gently so that the peas swish around in a circle.

(b) thunder — a cookie sheet
   Hold the sheet by one corner and shake it.

(c) fire — a piece of stiff cellophane
   Crumple the cellophane in your hands.

(d) a train — two sandpaper blocks
   Rub the blocks together, going faster and faster

(e) hoofbeats — two coconut shells or two small wooden salad bowls
   Drum them on a floor or other hard surface with a cloppity-clop rhythm.

(f) footsteps in the snow—a plastic bag filled with flour.
Slap the bag against a hard surface, a footstep rhythm.
(Make sure that the bag is strong and that it is tightly
tied—otherwise, you'll have a flour shower!)

(g) jackhammer—typewriter
Insert a paper in the typewriter. With two fingers, hit any two keys
rapidly. Or with an electric typewriter, hold down one of the repeater
keys.

(h) jet plane—a hairdryer

(i) voice on the telephone—a small plastic cup
Speak into the cup.

What to Do:

1. Choose the story you want to tape. You might read your favorite story onto the tape, putting in sound effects where they are needed. Or you might write an adventure play with dialogue for you and your friends.

2. The effects listed above will get you started. Once you start to think about how things sound, you'll find lots of other good sound effects around the house. You can probably make some with your voice, too. Can you imitate a creaking door? A car screeching to a stop? (You'd better practice where you won't bother anyone else!)

3. Bring all your sound effects supplies together. Arrange them (maybe on a table top) in the

order you'll need them. If you have written out your play, mark where the sound effects come in. One or two people should take care of the sound effects while the others read their parts. Have a couple of practice run-throughs before you turn on the tape recorder.

Eye Spy

Do you believe you can see around corners? And over walls that are taller than you are? With a periscope, you can.

What You Need:
scissors or pen knife
an empty milk carton, 1 quart (1 L) size
2 pocket-size mirrors
adhesive tape
a square piece of cardboard (same size as top of milk carton)

What to Do:

1. Wash out the milk carton. (Or you'll find out that old, sour milk smells awful!) The next steps are a bit tricky. Ask an adult to help you cut the carton and put in the mirrors.

DRAWING 1.

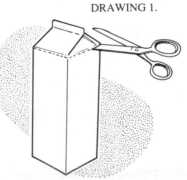

2. Cut the top off the carton *(drawing 1)*.

DRAWING 2.

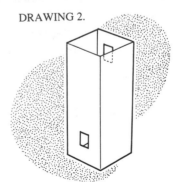

3. Cut holes in the carton as shown in drawing 2. One hole is in the *back* of the carton, about 2 inches (5 cm) from the top. The other hole is in the *front* of the carton, about 2 inches (5 cm) from the bottom.

4. Put the mirrors into the carton. Start with the bottom mirror. The mirror should have its shiny side facing *up*. Tape it into the carton at a 45° angle, as shown in drawing 3.

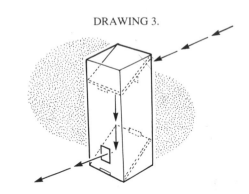

DRAWING 3.

5. Put the second mirror at the top of the carton. The second mirror should have its shiny side facing *down*. It should also be at a 45° angle. *(See drawing 3.)* Tape it in place.

6. When the mirrors are arranged, put the piece of cardboard over the top of the carton. Tape it in place.

7. Take your periscope to a corner. Hold it so that the top hole is sticking out past the corner. Look through the bottom hole. What do you see? You can also use the periscope to see over high walls.

New Hope for Deaf People

Some people with hearing problems have middle ears that don't carry sounds properly. They can often be helped with hearing aids. Other people, though, are deaf because their inner ears are damaged. Until very recently, there was no way to aid them. Now there is an invention that can help these people. It's called a *cochlear implant*. Electrical wires are put right into the cochlea so that sound messages can be sent to the brain. These sounds are not like the ones normal ears can hear. People with cochlear implants have to work very hard to learn what the sounds mean. Some of them have even learned to understand what other people are saying.

Index

Braille *16*

Cochlear implant *95*

Ears, and balance *79*
    cochlea *60*
    ear canal *59*
    eardrum *59-60, 61*
    hammer, anvil, stirrup *60*
    inner ear *60*
    middle ear *59, 61*
    oval window *60*
    pinnae *59*
    sacculi, utricle *79*
    semicircular canals *79*

Echolocation *73*

Extra-sensory perception *80*
    precognition *80*
    telepathy *80, 82*

Eyes, and after-images *50, 55*
    blind spot *58*
    cones *48, 50*
    cornea *36*
    iris *36*
    lens *37*
    pupil *36-37*
    retina *48*
    rods *48, 50*

Indian moon moth *26*

Giant squid *47*

Krakatoa *61*

Nerves, pain receptors *9*
    sense receptors *8*
    temperature receptors *8*
    touch receptors *8*
    number of *16*

Senses, and inventions *87-89*

Skin, and formation *11*
    dermis *7*
    epidermis *7*

Smell, and nose *17*
    molecules and *17-18*
    nerve messages and *18*

Something To Do
    Amazing Animation *42-44*
    An Orange-Clove Pomander
        Ball *22*
    Bone Tones *65*
    Can You Find Your Own
        Nose? *86*
    Colorful After-Images *55*
    Eye Spy *93-94*
    Gee Whiz — It's Fizz *23*
    Get the Point? *10-11*
    Good Vibrations *74-75*
    Great Grandma's Gramo-
        phone *62-63*
    Hear, There and Every-
        where *64*
    How Dizzy Can You
        Get? *81*
    How Much Touch? *12-13*
    In a Spin *51-53*

Make It Sweeter—with
    Salt! *33*
Make Your Own
    Rainbow *54*
Map Your Tongue *32*
Oven Rack Chimes *66*
Phantom Colors *56-57*
Roses for Noses *20-21*
Secret Messages *76-77*
See Some Sounds *70-71*
Seeing Things (That Aren't
    There!) *40-41*
Soup's On *24-25*
Spooky Trees *46*
Sugar, Spice ... and
    Everything Nice *34*
Take a Taste Test *30-31*
Temperature Trick *14*
Thrilling Sound
    Effects *90-92*
Tick Tricks *72*
Try Some Telepathy *82*
Two Senses' Worth *84*
Weird Wetness *15*
What's a Thaumatrope? *45*

Sound, and loudness *69*
    and pitch *69*
    and sound waves *68*

Spectrum *48, 51, 54*

Synesthesia *85*

Taste, and nose *28*
    taste buds *28*
    tongue *28-29*

Ultrasound *69, 89*

HAVE MORE FUN WITH SCIENCE...

JOIN THE SCIENCE FOR EVERY KID CLUB

Tell Us About Your Favorite Experiment And Receive A Free Gift!

Just fill in the coupon below and mail to:
FAN CLUB HEADQUARTERS/F. Nachbaur
John Wiley & Sons, 605 Third Avenue, New York, NY 10158
(Attach a separate sheet for experiment)

- -

Name_____
Address_____
City_____State_____ Zip_____
Age_____

Would you be interested in joining the *Science for Every Kid Club*?
YES_____   NO_____

Where did you buy this book? _____
What other books do you enjoy reading?_____

Membership in the *Science for Every Kid Club* entitles you to the official
membership card, newsletters, and other surprises...and it's free!!!

WILEY
Publishers Since 1807

001